It's My Body

Arms and Hands

Lola Schaefer

Raintree

www.raintreepublishers.co.uk

Visit our website to find out more information about **Raintree** books.

To order:
- ☎ Phone 44 (0) 1865 888112
- 📄 Send a fax to 44 (0) 1865 314091
- 💻 Visit the Raintree Bookshop at **www.raintreepublishers.co.uk** to browse our catalogue and order online.

First published in Great Britain by Raintree, Halley Court, Jordan Hill, Oxford OX2 8EJ, part of Harcourt Education.
Raintree is a registered trademark of Harcourt Education Ltd.

Editorial: Jennifer Gillis and Diyan Leake
Design: Sue Emerson and Michelle Lisseter
Picture Research: Jennifer Gillis
Production: Lorraine Hicks

Originated by Dot Gradations
Printed and bound in China by South China Printing Company

ISBN 1 844 21647 0
07 06 05 04 03
10 9 8 7 6 5 4 3 2 1

British Library Cataloguing in Publication Data
Schaefer, Lola
Arms and hands
612.9'7
A full catalogue record for this book is available from the British Library.

Acknowledgements
The publishers would like to thank the following for permission to reproduce photographs: Corbis p. 7 (Left Lane Productions); Custom Medical Stock Photo pp. 10, 23 (bone, knuckle); Heinemann Library pp. 4 (Robert Lifson), 6 (Brian Warling), 8 (Robert Lifson), 9 (Brian Warling), 12 (Brian Warling), 13 (Brian Warling), 14 (Brian Warling), 15 (Brian Warling), 16 (Brian Warling), 17 (Brian Warling), 20 (Robert Lifson), 21 (Brian Warling), 22 (Brian Warling), 23 (elbow, palm, muscle, Brian Warling), 24 (Brian Warling); PhotoEdit p. 5 (Jose Carillo); PhotoTake (Collection CNRI) pp. 18, 23 (joint).

Cover photograph reproduced with permission of Getty images/Taxi.

Every effort has been made to contact copyright holders of any material reproduced in this book. Any omissions will be rectified in subsequent printings if notice is given to the publishers.

Some words are shown in bold, **like this**. You can find them in the glossary on page 23.

Contents

What are my arms and hands?

Arms and hands are parts of your body.

Your body is made up of many parts.

Each part of your body does a job.

Arms and hands help you lift, hold and carry.

Where are my arms?

arm

Your arms rest at the sides of your body.

They are **limbs** joined to your body at your shoulders.

Shoulders are **joints** that help your arms move.

What do my arms look like?

Arms are covered in smooth skin.

You can stretch them up straight.

You can bend your arms to look like the letters V or L.

What is inside my arms?

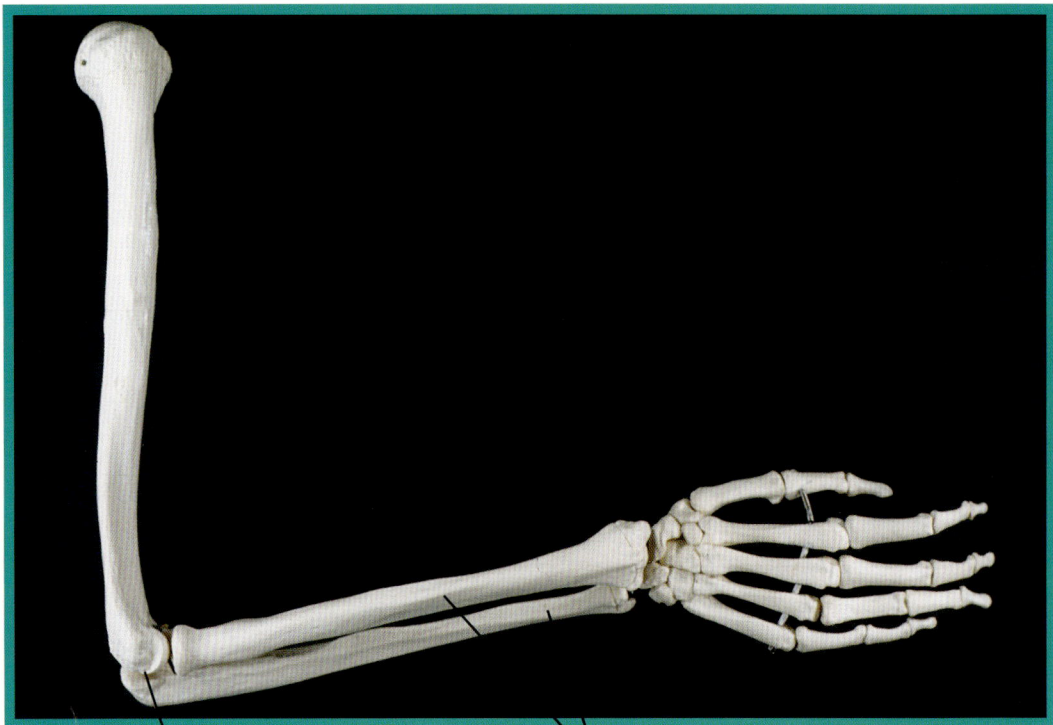

elbow | bones

There are **bones** inside your arms.

Your arm bones meet at your **elbow**.

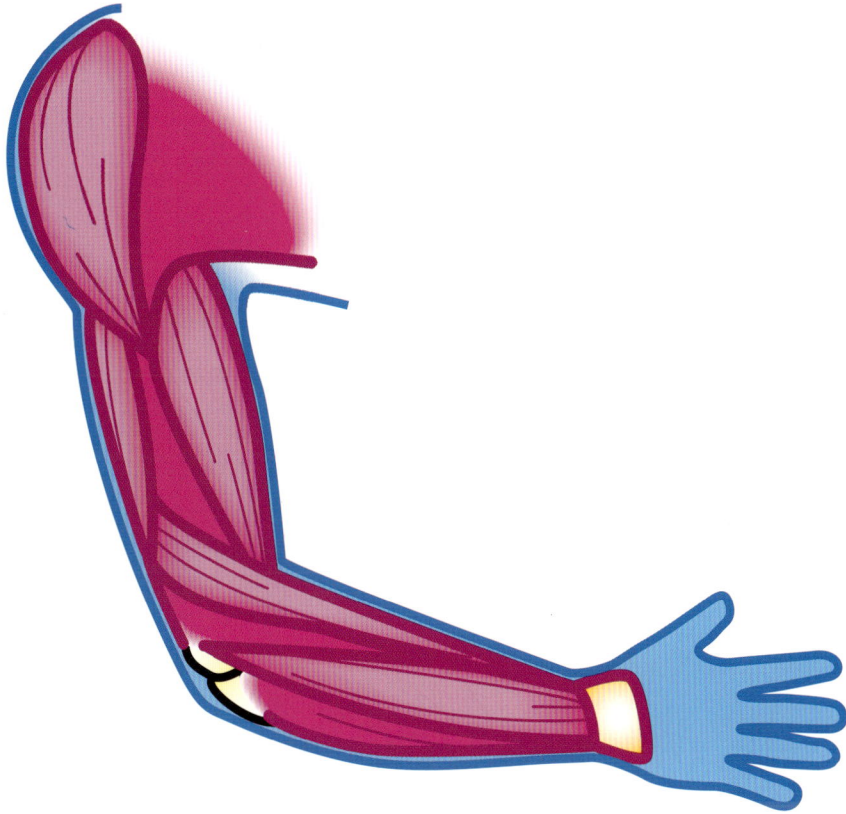

There are **muscles** inside your arms.

You use your muscles to move your **joints** and bones.

What can I do with my arms?

Your arms help you lift.

You can carry big things.

You use your arms to hold things.

You can put your arms around the people you love.

Where are my hands?

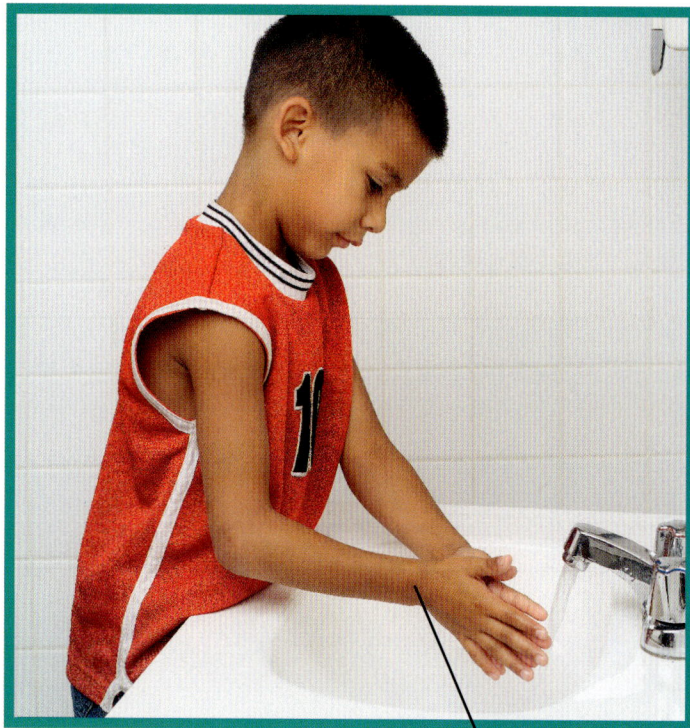

wrist

Your hands are at the ends of your arms.

Wrists join your hands to your arms.

Wrists are **joints** that help your hands move.

What do my hands look like?

Hands have four fingers and one thumb.

Thumbs can move to help you pick things up.

Your hands are covered in skin.

Your **palm** is the soft front part of your hand.

What is inside my hands?

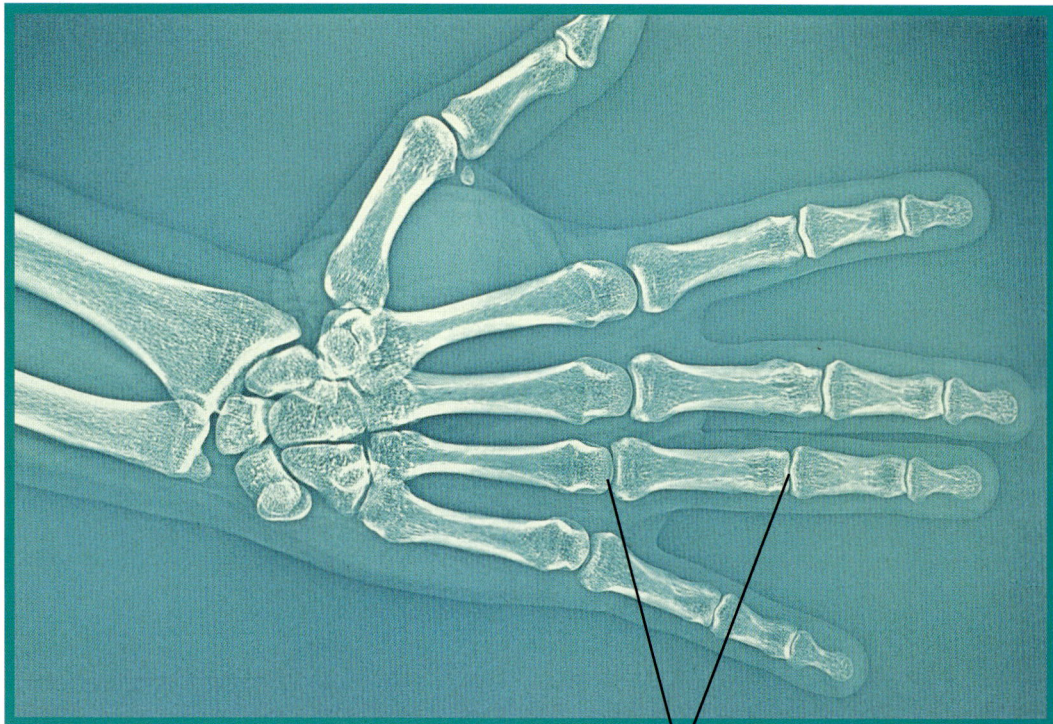

knuckles

There are **bones** inside your hands.

Some of the bones fit together at **joints** called **knuckles**.

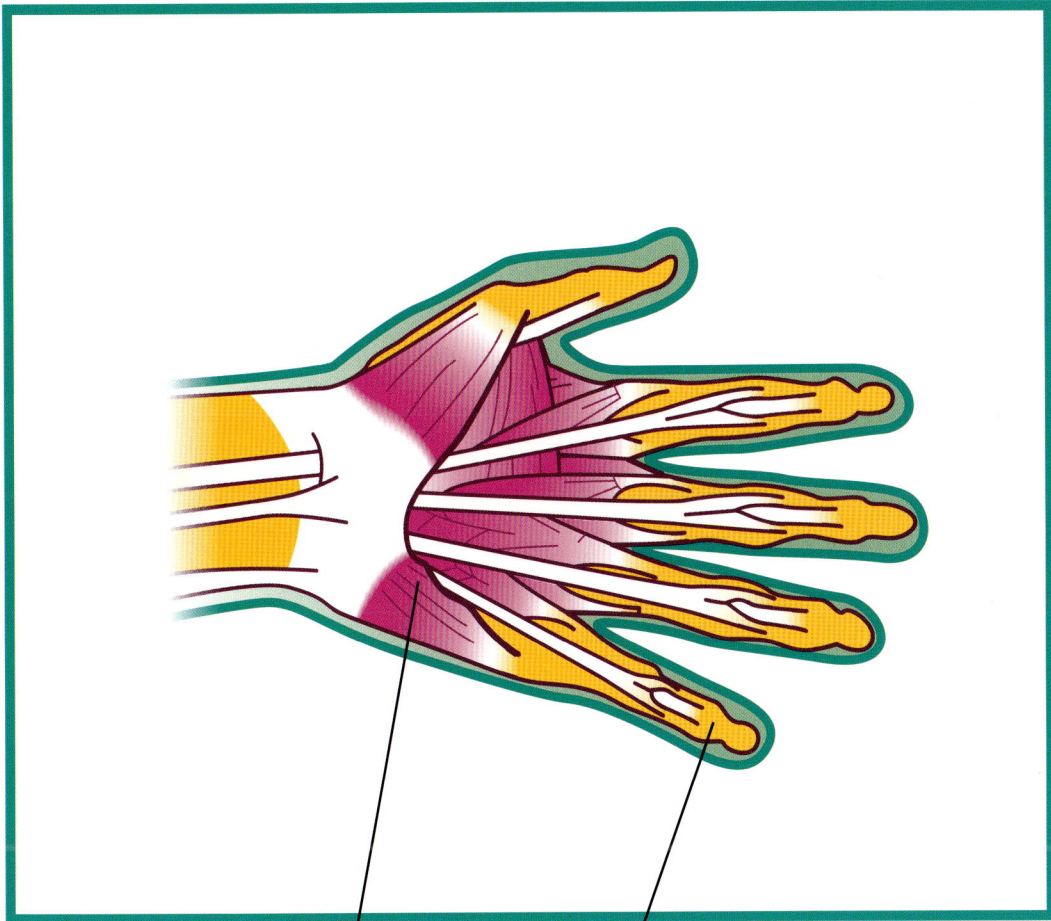

muscles   bone

You use your **muscles** to move your fingers and thumb around.

The muscles pull the bones.

What can I do with my hands?

You can touch and feel things with your hands.

You can hold another hand.

You can pick up crayons with your hands.

You can catch, hold or carry things.

Quiz

Do you know what these are?

Look for the answers on page 24.

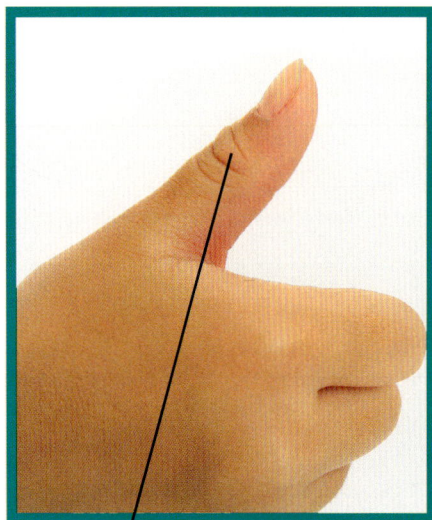

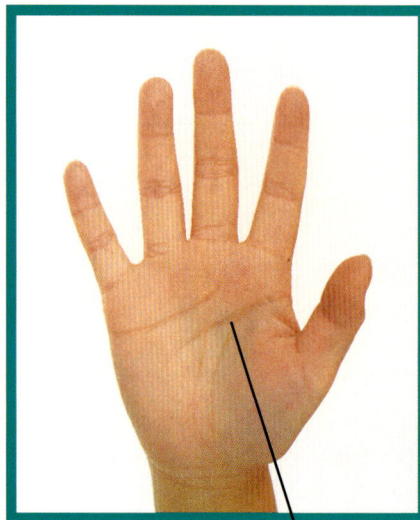

?

?

?

Glossary

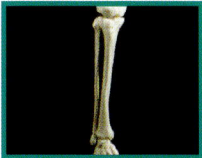
bone
hard part inside your body

elbow
the joint in your arm

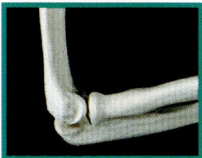
joint
a part of your body where bones come together so they can move

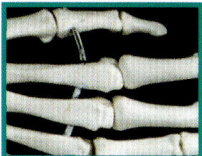
knuckles
the joints in your fingers

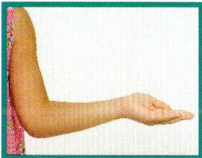
limb
arm or leg

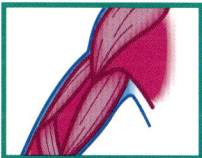
muscle
a part in your body that you use to move with

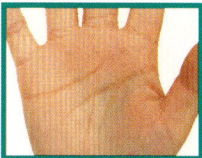
palm
the soft front part of your hand

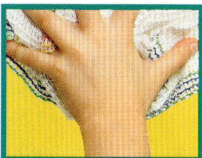
wrist
the body part where your arm joins your hand

Index

Answers to quiz on page 22

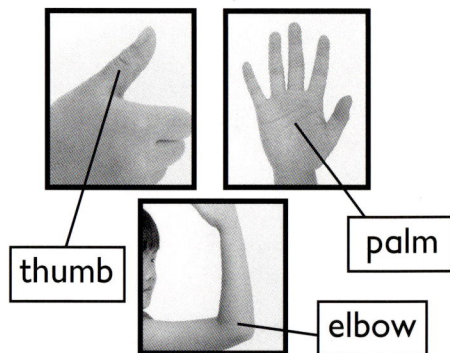

thumb

palm

elbow

24

Titles in the It's My Body series include:

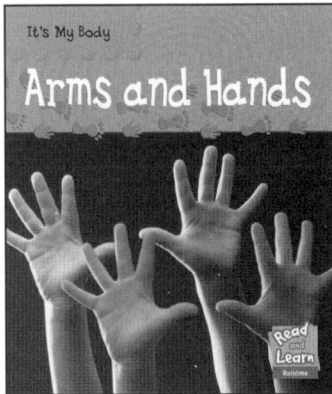

It's My Body
Arms and Hands

Hardback   1 844 21647 0

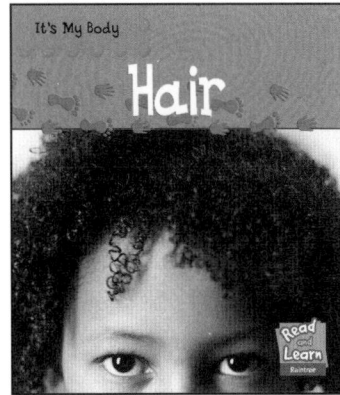

It's My Body
Hair

Hardback   1 844 21648 9

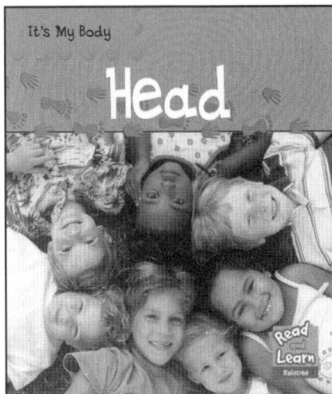

It's My Body
Head

Hardback   1 844 21649 7

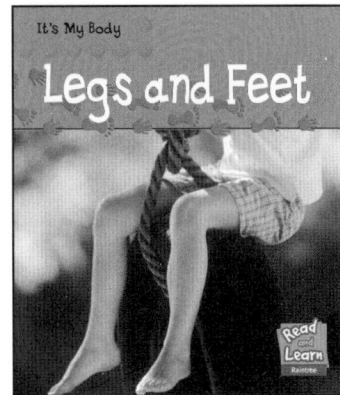

It's My Body
Legs and Feet

Hardback   1 844 21650 0

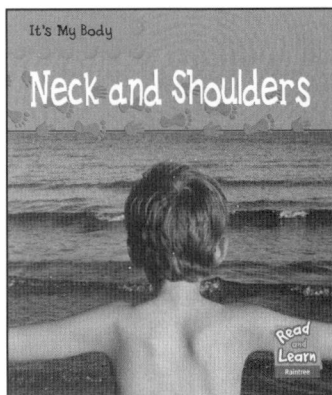

It's My Body
Neck and Shoulders

Hardback   1 844 21651 9

Find out about the other titles in this series on our website www.raintreepublishers.co.uk